I0139486

ANATOMY OF A HUG

Kat Ramsburg

BROADWAY PLAY PUBLISHING INC
New York
www.broadwayplaypublishing.com
info@broadwayplaypublishing.com

ANATOMY OF A HUG
© Copyright 2020 Kat Ramsburg

All rights reserved. This work is fully protected under the copyright laws of the United States of America. No part of this publication may be photocopied, reproduced, stored in a retrieval system, or transmitted, in any form or by any means, electronic, mechanical, recording, or otherwise, without the prior permission of the publisher. Additional copies of this play are available from the publisher.

Written permission is required for live performance of any sort. This includes readings, cuttings, scenes, and excerpts. For amateur and stock performances, please contact Broadway Play Publishing Inc. For all other rights please contact the author c/o B P P I.

Cover art courtesy of Jason Glick

First edition: November 2020
I S B N: 978-0-88145-883-1

Book design: Marie Donovan
Page make-up: Adobe InDesign
Typeface: Palatino

ANATOMY OF A HUG was developed by ESPA: Primary Stages and the Great Plains Theatre Conference. It received its Developmental Premiere at the Bridge Initiative (Director, Amanda Trombley).

ANATOMY OF A HUG received its World Premiere at Trustus Theatre on 19 August 2016. The cast and creative contributor were:

AMELIA..Rebecca Williams
BEN ....Patrick Michael Kelly
SONIA..Dewey Scott-Wiley
IRIS .... Annette Grevious

Director... Chad Henderson

CHARACTERS & SETTING

AMELIA, (F), *early/mid 30s. Any ethnicity. As nondescript as IKEA furniture. Subtle and fragile. Lives vicariously through her beloved television characters.*

SONIA, *(F), mid/late 50s. Any ethnicity. Weathered, hard, but somehow full of life, which is odd since she's dying.*

BEN, (M), *mid 30s. Any ethnicity. Could easily be confused with the underdog character from a sit-com.*

IRIS, *(F), early 50s. African American. A spirited mother earth type. Large in stature, presence, and hope.*

The play allows for diverse casting. It takes place in Seattle, where there is a rich tapestry of ethnicities, particularly, Black, Latinx, Asian Americans, and Indigenous people. Please make every effort to reflect this diversity in your casting choices.

Time: Present.

Place: Seattle.

NOTES

/ indicates the next line should begin.

The typos in the Pledge of Allegiance are intentional, and should be read as written.

A THOUGHT ON THE DIRECTION & DESIGN

I envision the set to look like a television sound stage. Amelia can walk from one location to another with no need for blackouts or elaborate transitions. It's not really a sit-com, of course, but that's the lens through which Amelia views the world. No other characters are aware of this lens. Feel free to play with the television aspect of the design, as much or as little as you see fit.

Lost

(A small apartment. Nothing nicer than IKEA. An effort has been made to make it homey, but it remains rather impersonal. There is a giant L C D television, which seems out of place and is taking up too much room. The T V is on. It's always on. AMELIA stands in the living room, SONIA sits in a cheap rented wheelchair. IRIS, is trying to fill the silence.)

IRIS: Isn't it nice, Sonia? I told you it was nice. Very homey. *(To AMELIA)* It was a beautiful drive too. We stopped for lunch over on the peninsula. Overlooking the water. One of those perfect Seattle days they never show on T V. Always with the rain… *(Pause)* Well, you've got my cell and the agency's number if you need anything. And I mean it. Anything. *(Beat)* Alright then. I'll leave you two to get to know each other. Give me a call later tonight and let me know how it's going. I think this is going to be a really good thing…for the both of you.

(IRIS exits. The women continue to stare at each other. After a moment)

AMELIA: *(A bit formally)* You can put your clothes in the hall closet. Do you have…?

SONIA: This is it.

AMELIA: I don't think I have anything that will—maybe I can check the lost and found at work.

SONIA: Thank you.

AMELIA: The bed didn't get here yet. Hopefully tomorrow. You'll have to sleep on the couch for now.

SONIA: Don't rearrange everything for me, Amy.

AMELIA: It's Amelia. That's the T V. Obviously. I have cable, D V R, Netflix and Hulu.

SONIA: Netflix?

AMELIA: The D V R records my favorite shows. Netflix is good for old movies, like early 2000s, and a lot of their original T V shows are pretty good. Hulu is good for shows you like, but don't love enough to D V R. They're all on the Roku, which also has Amazon Prime, Showtime and H B O. *(Beat)* Bathroom's down there. Kitchen. Help yourself to whatever. I don't know what you like to eat.

SONIA: Anything is fine.

AMELIA: People say that, but there's always something.

SONIA: Really. Anything.

AMELIA: You can't hurt my feelings.

(Beat)

SONIA: I don't really like bologna.

AMELIA: See? Now I won't buy bologna.

SONIA: But if you want / bolo—

AMELIA: I don't. *(Beat)* Can you walk?

SONIA: I can get around.

AMELIA: I'll ask about a walker.

SONIA: Where do you sleep?

AMELIA: Past the bathroom. My room's off limits okay?

SONIA: Yeah. Okay.

AMELIA: I'm not hiding anything.

SONIA: You need something that's your own. I get it.

(Beat)

AMELIA: So that's the whole tour.

SONIA: Can I sit on the couch?

AMELIA: Yeah. Sorry.
(She tries to help, but without ever actually touching
SONIA.*)*
Do you want some water? Or juice? It's not fresh. It's
that frozen kind.

SONIA: Water.

*(*AMELIA *goes to the kitchen.)*

SONIA: Do you have ice cubes?

AMELIA: *(O S)* Um, yeah?

SONIA: Can I have some?

AMELIA: *(O S)* Sure. *(Beat)* How many?

SONIA: Fill it up. Let the water fill in the gaps. *(Beat)*
The things you miss. You wouldn't think ice cubes
would be on that list.

(No response)

SONIA: How long have you lived here?

AMELIA: *(O S)* Two years, maybe?

SONIA: You own it?

*(*AMELIA *re-enters.)*

AMELIA: I don't know if we should share personal
information.

SONIA: I'm just asking about your apartment.

AMELIA: *(It takes a second to come up with…)* My friends,
Lily and Marshall, used to live here. They bought a
place and so I moved in.

SONIA: It's nice. When Iris described it—

AMELIA: Iris?

SONIA: *(Indicating the door)* Iris.

AMELIA: Ms Owen?

SONIA: Yes. Can I put my feet up on the couch? They swell.

AMELIA: It's just IKEA.

(SONIA doesn't know what that is.)

AMELIA: It's a furniture store. And they sell meatballs.

SONIA: It's comfy.

AMELIA: The catalogue is cool.

(AMELIA hands SONIA an IKEA catalogue and then helps her put her feet up on the couch, again, without making physical contact.)

SONIA: It's all imported.

AMELIA: But it's not like nice or—. You should go sometime. There's lots to see. Couches, plates, lamps.

SONIA: *(Noting the catalogue)* Small blonde children.

(AMELIA almost laughs but then stops herself. SONIA sees the opening and takes it.)

SONIA: Amelia…Amy. / Sweetie.

AMELIA: No. Uh, uh. No.
(She exits to the kitchen.)

SONIA: Alright.

(Transition)

Friends

(AMELIA is at work. It's a cubicle with very few signs that would indicate anything about Amelia's personality or how long she's been at the job. She is finishing a call when BEN, a gregarious co-worker, walks up. He has a small plant.)

AMELIA: *(On the phone)* You'll receive a photo of your sponsored child in the mail within five to seven days. Thank you for joining the, International Children are Our Family, family.

(She hangs up.)

BEN: Happy anniversary!

AMELIA: Anniv—?

BEN: Three years!

AMELIA: Really?

BEN: LouAnne made a pie. It's in the break room.

AMELIA: That was nice of her.

BEN: We had a secret staff meeting and guessed what kind you would like.

AMELIA: Oh.

BEN: Do you want to know what kind we chose?

AMELIA: Um, sure?

BEN: Lemon meringue!

AMELIA: That…sounds good.

BEN: But LouAnne said meringue was too hard to transport on the bus, so she made apple instead.

AMELIA: That also sounds good.

BEN: It's got a cinnamon crumble.

AMELIA: Even better.

BEN: You like pie, right?

AMELIA: *(Doesn't know how to break it to him)* I'm sure everyone else will enjoy it.

BEN: Nooooooo! Seriously? There was a twenty-minute discussion about whether you were a pie or cake kind of gal. I really thought we nailed it.

AMELIA: For what it's worth, I'm not really a cake gal either.

BEN: Good to know! I'll add it to Amelia's List of Facts.

AMELIA: You keep a list of facts about me?

BEN: Not a physical list, per se, more like, a mental note.

AMELIA: Why?

BEN: You're an enigma.

AMELIA: An enigma?

BEN: A mystery.

AMELIA: I know what enig—I'm not mysterious. I'm just…a person.

BEN: I find you very interesting.

AMELIA: That's weird.

BEN: No. No. You don't see what I see.

AMELIA: Which is?

BEN: Someone who sits there, day after day, with a quiet determination to feed all the children of Burundi.

AMELIA: And that makes me interesting?

BEN: Someone so optimistic about life that they are completely happy at their slightly above minimum wage job.

AMELIA: Yeah…you're strange.

BEN: Oh come on! I keep facts in my head about lots of people.
(Pointing out a co-worker.)
Phillip, over in Haiti, has three cats, plays indoor soccer on Wednesdays, and spends every lunch hour at Taco Time.

AMELIA: Do you have that Asperger's thing?

BEN: *(Sincerely)* What? No. I—I'm just trying to— I just wanted to— Ahhhh. Yeah, this did not go the way it did in my head. *(To himself)* You just said that out loud Ben.

AMELIA: *(Throwing him a bone)* How many facts do you have about me?

BEN: Let's see. Uh… One. You work here. Two. You take the Number 5 that arrives at 8:47 A M and departs at 5:09 P M. And I only know that because I ride the same bus.

AMELIA: You do?

BEN: I do. Three. You keep your desk very clean. Four. You prefer tea over coffee, which makes you an anomaly among Seattleites.

AMELIA: These are really interesting facts you've compiled.

BEN: Those were early on. They get juicier. You take your lunch at one pm everyday, without fail. You don't like pie or cake!

AMELIA: You're basically Magnum P I.

BEN: And you have the best co-worker on the planet. Happy anniversary.

(BEN hands AMELIA the plant.)

AMELIA: Um. Thanks.

BEN: I know you don't like to keep things on your desk. Another fact. But I thought a plant isn't really a thing. It's alive. You have to care for it. So it's more like a person than a thing.

AMELIA: You really believe that?

BEN: I do! And I think that people aren't really your thing either. Am I right? *(Beat)* Sorry. That was—so anyway, I thought a plant would—

AMELIA: Are you going to be totally devastated when I accidentally kill it?

BEN: *(Taking back the plant)* Shhhhhh! She can hear.

AMELIA: Plants can't hear.

BEN: *(To the plant)* Don't listen to her. She's a non-believer.

AMELIA: So…uh. What do you do here?

BEN: Seriously?

AMELIA: I don't get out of Africa much.

BEN: *(Trying to crack a joke)* Even Meryl had to leave eventually.

(AMELIA has no idea what he's talking about.)

BEN: Oh come on! You've never seen *Out of Africa?* Hands down one of my top five films.

AMELIA: I'm more into T V than movies.

BEN: Huh. Now I have another fact! *(Beat)* I'm in that pod, over there. India and Nepal.

AMELIA: You guys seem like you have a lot of fun.

BEN: Oh it's always a party in India and Nepal. Plus I'm a pretty awesome manager.

AMELIA: And confident.

BEN: I guess I am. Is that why you don't talk to me in the break room?

AMELIA: Huh?

BEN: I thought you were just shy or something, and that sooner or later, I'd break through. But, oh man! You've been thinking I'm a narcissistic dweeb this whole time.

AMELIA: No! I've never thought…that…about you. I promise.

BEN: Really?

AMELIA: Truly.

BEN: *(To the plant)* We still have a chance Plantasia!

AMELIA: Plantasia?

BEN: You can rename her. I just thought the name gave her a bit of personality.

(AMELIA almost laughs.)

BEN: You think I'm funny!

AMELIA: I think anyone who names inanimate objects is funny.

BEN: I'm beginning to rethink leaving Plantasia with you.

AMELIA: It would be a strong choice on your part to take it, um, *her*, with you. Not that I don't appreciate the gesture.

BEN: Another fact. Doesn't like plants.

AMELIA: No! I just have too much respect for… Plantasia…to let her die a slow, dehydrated death.

BEN: How about this? I'm going to leave her with you, but I'll stop by once a day to water her and chat with you.

(When AMELIA doesn't agree…)

BEN: That's the deal. Plantasia shouldn't have to grow up without a mother.

AMELIA: *(Her wall is back up.)* I should really get back on the phone. There are starving children in Burundi. I need to find sponsors for them before…you know.

BEN: I'll let you get back to saving the world. *(Beat)* It was nice talking with you.

AMELIA: You too.

(BEN begins to walk away but stops.)

BEN: I've been building up the courage to talk to you since I started working here. This morning, on the bus, I thought, "Today's the day Ben. You can do this!" So I stopped at Pike Place to get this plant. I thought it would make a nice ice-breaker. The guy at the stand said you would probably prefer flowers, but I think I know you a little better than he does. As I walked back up the hill to the office I thought, "What are you doing Ben?" but then quickly convinced myself to go through with it. Honestly, I don't think I could go another day wondering if you think about me half as often as I think about you.

AMELIA: Oh. Um—

BEN: I'm telling you all of this right now, because if you don't want me to ever talk to you again, I can handle it. I can go back to India and you can stay in Burundi and we can pretend this never happened.

AMELIA: That would probably / be for the best.

BEN: But maybe there's a little part of you that finds me interesting. Maybe you've been building up the courage to talk to *me* as well. Maybe you gave yourself the *same* pep talk on the bus this morning. Maybe today, at lunch, you would have looked up from your peanut butter and honey on whole wheat and said "Hi, Ben." *(Beat)* Anyway, I wasn't sure how it would happen, but I knew today was the day we would talk.

AMELIA: *(Gently defensive)* Was it everything you imagined it to be?

BEN: We'll get there.
(He begins to walk away again but stops.)
What's your favorite T V show of all time?

AMELIA: *Punky Brewster.*

BEN: *Freaks and Geeks.*

AMELIA: That's a good one too.

BEN: And now you have a fact about me.

(BEN *sets* Plantasia *on* AMELIA'*s desk and exits.*)

(*Transition*)

Three's Company

(*Outside* AMELIA'*s apartment. She is carrying a reusable shopping bag full of groceries.* IRIS *approaches her.*)

IRIS: Can I help?

AMELIA: I've got it.

IRIS: Here, let me take the bags.

AMELIA: I didn't realize you would still be in the picture.

IRIS: We like to make sure—

AMELIA: We?

IRIS: My agency.

AMELIA: How come I've only met you?

IRIS: I'm your mother's caseworker—your *family's* caseworker. You should feel free to call me when—

AMELIA: You're just gonna stop by whenever?

IRIS: Sonia invited me over for dinner. She didn't—?

AMELIA: No.

IRIS: How has it been, having your mom back?

AMELIA: Lots of girl-talk, painting each other's nails, braiding our hair.

IRIS: You did the right thing Amelia. You and your momma are going to come out stronger than—

AMELIA: You seem to be under the impression that we were a happy family waiting to be reunited.

IRIS: I know it's a complicated situation, but getting your mom back, even for a few months—you may begin to realize how much you've wanted this.

AMELIA: Yes, all those years, hoping for a big, happy reunion.

IRIS: There's no reason to get defensive with me Amelia. I'm your advocate too.

(AMELIA *scoffs*.)

IRIS:Compassionate Release is rarely granted. There are many families who would love to be in your shoes right now.

AMELIA: *(Pointed)* Really? Would they?

IRIS: There are a lot of folks keeping an eye on your case. My agency wants this to work.

AMELIA: And I'm not cooperating very well.

IRIS: There's no right or wrong way to do this Amelia. Everything you're feeling is valid. But being open to how you might change—.

AMELIA: I've gone through plenty of change, being moved from foster home to foster home. I don't want to change anymore. This is my home. Those are my things in there. And now everything is— And I don't like it when things are— You didn't tell me it would feel like this.

IRIS: This is new territory for both of us. I wish I could have prepared you better, but there's not a lot of research on this type of reunion.

AMELIA: Wait. We're your guinea pigs?

IRIS: No. You're—

AMELIA: You made it sound like this is what people do.

IRIS: I've been helping families connect through letters and visitations for years, but Compassionate Release—it's new to me.

AMELIA: So you throw us in a house together like *Big Brother*?

IRIS: No!

AMELIA: Like I'm Izzie Stevens, or something!

IRIS: Look, I met Sonia and in all the years I've worked with—

AMELIA: Murderers.

IRIS: The *incarcerated*—I've never been more certain, that woman didn't belong in the system. I hoped you would see the same thing in her.

AMELIA: She killed my father, and meant to kill me.

IRIS: She meant to kill herself.

AMELIA: She should have tried harder!

IRIS: Don't say that. You don't mean that.

AMELIA: You don't know anything about me.

IRIS: This is your opportunity to deal with all of your unresolved issues with your mom.

AMELIA: I moved on.

IRIS: No one moves on from something like that. Not without extensive therapy.

AMELIA: Child Services doesn't exactly provide top quality care.

IRIS: I understand that. But now you have a chance to ask the questions that have been eating away at you. You deserve to know what really happened. And Sonia deserves to—

AMELIA: You don't get to decide what she deserves.

(Beat)

IRIS: You know Amelia, I've been sober for seventeen years, which means I wasn't sober for many years before that. My husband left me. I lost my psychiatry practice. My daughter dealt with me being a drunk by being an over achiever. She's a doctor now. But my son—he's over in Central Penitentiary.

AMELIA: So you set criminals free to make up for your failure as a parent?

IRIS: I understand that not everyone in prison is there because they are inherently bad. There are extenuating circumstances that—

AMELIA: Did she convince you that she's the victim?

IRIS: She accepts full responsibility.

AMELIA: She's somehow convinced you she deserves a better life than rotting in prison!

IRIS: It's not my job to decide whether someone is innocent or guilty. I'm just here to see that—

AMELIA: They die with dignity.

IRIS: No. Those are the euthanasia people.

(Beat)

AMELIA: I did my part, Ms. Owen. I helped you get her out. But don't expect me to play house.

IRIS: You returned my call. You said yes.

AMELIA: You're very persuasive.

IRIS: Amelia, whatever your reasons were for taking her in, just know, they might change. You may find that the woman you've grown to hate over these years isn't the woman you've allowed into your home.

AMELIA: I will never stop hating her.

IRIS: I'm not asking you to. I'm just asking you to open up about how her actions affected you.

AMELIA: Like she cares.

IRIS: She does. I promise you, she does. *(Beat)* Amelia, stage four ovarian cancer means—

AMELIA: I know what it means.
(Pause. Shift. Holding up an Amazon box)
Murphy Brown came in the mail today. So if you want to come in and keep Sonia company while I—.

IRIS: I would like that. Thank you.

(AMELIA unlocks the door. A hospital bed now takes up much of the living room making it even more crowded. SONIA is asleep. She is wearing oxygen.)

IRIS: Should someone be with her during the day?

AMELIA: The hospice nurse stops by every day. Sonia talks her ear off.

IRIS: I'm sure she does.

AMELIA: Tomato or split pea?

IRIS: I don't want to be any trouble.

AMELIA: *(To herself)* That ship has sailed.

(AMELIA goes to the kitchen. SONIA begins to wake up.)

SONIA: Iris.

IRIS: Hi, Sonia.

AMELIA: She came for dinner.

SONIA: I know. I invited her.

AMELIA: You gotta tell me these things. Here're your meds.

SONIA: Take out the morphine.

AMELIA: You're going to regret—

SONIA: I don't want to be doped up while Iris is here.

IRIS: Don't worry about me. Pop those pills.

(SONIA *does.* AMELIA *goes back to the kitchen. We hear a can opener, and eventually a microwave.*)

IRIS:You're looking much better.

SONIA: That's nice of you to say.

IRIS: How are you adjusting?

SONIA: Slowly.

IRIS: Have you gone outside? For a walk, at least?

SONIA: Amy works during the day.

IRIS: You need to get out there. See what you've been missing.

SONIA: (*Indicating the apartment*) This is a big enough adjustment.

IRIS: Better than D O C?

SONIA: It's different than I thought it would be.

IRIS: Transitioning takes time. You've been away for a long while.

SONIA: She didn't even visit me before she agreed to do this.

IRIS: This was the best scenario.

SONIA: For me. But she's making it pretty clear she doesn't want me here.

IRIS: She's made room for you. She's caring for you.

SONIA: I never understood her. She was always a strange kid.

IRIS: You need to get to know *this* Amelia.

(*Beat*)

SONIA: How are your kids? Wanna trade?

IRIS: Tamika's going to have her baby any day now.

SONIA: (*Teasing*) Grandma.

IRIS: Oooh. I'm not quite ready for that.

SONIA: They come whether we're ready or not.

IRIS: I'll bring pictures when he arrives.

SONIA: I'd like that.

IRIS: And I'll see about a volunteer therapist for you and Amelia. Maybe having someone else guiding the conversation will help.

SONIA: Can't you do it?

IRIS: It's better if it's someone neutral.

SONIA: Thanks, Iris.

IRIS: For what it's worth, you don't look a day over stage three.

(AMELIA *has been watching from the door.*)

AMELIA: How regularly will you be visiting us?

IRIS: As often as you need it. Once I feel like your family has—

AMELIA: This isn't a family. *(Beat)* This is a temporary—

IRIS: Amelia, we talked about being open.

AMELIA: *(To* SONIA*)* You've got three months left, right?

SONIA: More or less.

AMELIA: There we go then. *(To* IRIS*)* Can I get you something to drink Ms. Owen?

IRIS: I'm fine. Thank you.

(The microwave beeps. AMELIA *returns to the kitchen.)*

IRIS: *(To* SONIA*)* Give her time.

SONIA: Give who time?

IRIS: Amelia.

SONIA: Right. Damn. The meds kick in and…it's a free ride to fantasyland.

IRIS: All aboard the coo-coo train.

(*They share a genuine laugh.*)

SONIA: How'd you fix things with your kids?

IRIS: Forgiveness is an ongoing journey.

SONIA: I don't need her forgiveness. I just need to know that she's okay.

(AMELIA *enters with a tray with three bowls of soup.*)

AMELIA: Soup?

IRIS: Thank you Amelia. Smells great.

AMELIA: It's from a can.

SONIA: What's this shit?

AMELIA: Dinner.

SONIA: We eat at five-thirty.

AMELIA: We eat when I get home.

SONIA: You're always changing the fucking rules around here!

IRIS: Sonia. You're home now. With Amelia. Your daughter.

SONIA: My daughter? You know her?

IRIS: She's right here.

SONIA: Bullshit! She never comes to see me!

IRIS: She's here now. And she's brought you dinner.

(SONIA *takes a long look at* AMELIA.)

SONIA: I thought you'd be prettier.

AMELIA: Eat or the meds make you sick.

SONIA: I'm not hungry!

AMELIA: Whatever.

(AMELIA *begins to head for her bedroom.*)

IRIS: You don't want to eat with us?

AMELIA: No.

IRIS: She doesn't know what she's saying. She probably needs her meds adjusted.

SONIA: I can hear you talking about me.

IRIS: Why don't we watch *Murphy Brown?*

AMELIA: I don't want to / watch it with her.

SONIA: Who the hell is *Murphy Brown?*

IRIS: One of my all time favorite TV television characters!

SONIA: He sounds fine. Turn him on.

(Beat)

IRIS: Amelia… Your mother would like to watch television with you.

AMELIA: Fine. Just don't talk through it or anything.

IRIS: Deal.

AMELIA: And *he's* a *she*.

(Transition)

My So Called Life

*(*AMELIA *ul work.)*

AMELIA: *(On the phone)* I completely understand that times are tough right now, but thirty-five dollars a month is hardly… *(Listens)* We're talking about a dollar-sixteen a day. That's not even a cup of— *(Listens)* But just think, if you bring lunch from home, one day a week you can feed a child in Burundi for an entire month! *(Listens)* Are you in a Starbucks drive through? *(Listens)* I'm not sure if you're talking to me or to— *(Listens)* So, as I was saying, there's a child in

Burundi who would love to be a part of your family.
You can write letters. Send photos of your kids. And
a couple times a year, your child will write back! That
could be really fun for your family to receive those
letters. For thirty-five dollars a month, your child will
receive nutritious food, a uniform for school, as well
as community improvements that will help your child
and her family become self-sustaining. It's a really
wonderful way to let a child know that someone out
there knows she's alive, and wants the best for her.
(Listens) Oh wonderful! Let's select a child to join your
family.

(Transition)

Full House

*(Later that night. AMELIA's apartment. She and SONIA sit
on opposite sides of the couch. They are watching T V.)*

AMELIA: That's Jack. And the girl is Kate.

SONIA: The plane crash! That was…so real.

AMELIA: It's L C D.

SONIA: L C D?

AMELIA: There was this trivia thing I won. At the mall.

SONIA: It's big.

AMELIA: It's too big for the room, but I won it so…

(AMELIA and SONIA watch Lost.*)*

SONIA: What was the question?

AMELIA: Hm?

SONIA: That you won on?

AMELIA: "What did Kramer name his chicken?"

(SONIA has no idea.)

AMELIA: Little Jerry Seinfeld! They basically handed me the answer. Not that I didn't *know* the answer, but COME. ON. That's a two thousand dollar television! So I made them give me another question, just to prove I would have won no matter what.

SONIA: *(Prodding)* What was that question?

AMELIA: "Who is the first character we meet on *Gilligan's Island*?" Now that is a *great* question. *(Beat)* Even you should know this one.

(SONIA has no idea.)

AMELIA: The Skipper! You would think it would be Gilligan, but it's the Skipper. He says, "Hey Gilligan. Gilligan!"

SONIA: When did you get so into T V? You always liked to be outside.

(Beat)

AMELIA: I, um, lived with this family once. The Banks's. They were super rich. And their nephew, Will, lived there too. He was from West Philadelphia. Born and raised. Anyway, um, I didn't want to be in the way so I just, you know, watched a lot of T V.

SONIA: It's a nice T V. All your T V watching really paid off.

AMELIA: *(Indicating T V)* That's Sawyer! Probably my favorite.

SONIA: Do you have a favorite show?

(No response)

SONIA: *M*A*S*H** was my favorite.

AMELIA: You should watch it again.

SONIA: Why would I do that?

AMELIA: To check in on everyone. You can stream it. On the Internet? Which you don't know about.

SONIA: I know about the Internet, Amy. I'm not an idiot.

AMELIA: Did you have T V there?

SONIA: We had a T V in the main room. But the Latina girls always had it on those courtroom shows. Judge so-and-so.

AMELIA: So…you haven't seen any T V since you…

SONIA: I was a little busy making license plates.

(Off AMELIA'*s look:)*

SONIA: That was a joke.

AMELIA: *(Changing the subject)* Lucky for you I pretty much have every good show on D V D.

*(*AMELIA *opens a cupboard to reveal an extensive D V D collection of every T V show known to man.)*

AMELIA: I belong to this club.

SONIA: When do you meet?

AMELIA: Not that kind of—. You get to pick a D V D set each month and it's a lot less than if you get it at Target. Do you know about D V Ds?

SONIA: You'll have to show me.

AMELIA: It's easy. And most of these you can stream now. But I like owning the D V D. The characters are always there if I need them, you know? *(To the T V)* Oh, that's John Locke. Keep your eye on him.

SONIA: You always liked to give away the endings of things.

(Beat)

AMELIA: Can you—can you not say things like that?

*(*AMELIA *and* SONIA *watch the T V together.)*

SONIA: What do you do when you're not watching T V?

AMELIA: Go to work.

SONIA: But besides that?

AMELIA: Stuff.

SONIA: That Jack is a handsome man.

AMELIA: I guess.

SONIA: Or Sawyer? ...Or maybe Kate?

(No response)

SONIA: I always pictured you married by now—with a couple of kids.

AMELIA: *(Annoyed)* Nope.

SONIA: You seeing anyone?

AMELIA: No personal information.

SONIA: Someone will come along.

(Pause)

AMELIA: I have a boyfriend actually.

SONIA: Oh! What's his name?

AMELIA: Ben. So, I'm fine.

SONIA: How long have you—?

AMELIA: A while.

SONIA: He never comes over. Or calls.

AMELIA: He's really busy.

SONIA: But it's serious? Do you think you'll marry him?

AMELIA: It's too early to—

SONIA: Do you want to marry him?

AMELIA: We don't talk about—it's not like that.

SONIA: Is he married to someone else?

AMELIA: No! He wouldn't— He's perfect. He...loves plants.

SONIA: How'd you meet?

AMELIA: What do you mean?

SONIA: Where did you meet him? Work? A bar?

AMELIA: No. Um. *(Beat)* I went in to his furniture store.

SONIA: He sells furniture?

AMELIA: He *makes* furniture. And he sells it in his store. Which he owns.

SONIA: *(Regarding the furniture in the room)* Did he make any of this?

AMELIA: His stuff's really expensive.

SONIA: I see.

AMELIA: I walked in to his store and I saw him. He was wearing a blue denim shirt. And his dog ran up to me and started, uh, humping my leg.

SONIA: Oh!

AMELIA: So he came over to talk. And that was it. We've been dating ever since.

SONIA: He should come by for dinner one day.

AMELIA: I don't think he—

SONIA: You haven't told him about me.

AMELIA: *(Indicating the T V)* Oh! You can't miss this part. You'll need to know this for season three. Episode six or seven.

(AMELIA and SONIA watch the T V together. There's a knock at the door. AMELIA makes no effort to go to the door. After a second…)

SONIA: You gonna answer it? Maybe it's Ben?

AMELIA: It's not Ben.

(AMELIA looks through the peephole.)

SONIA: Well who is it?

AMELIA: Did you invite Ms Owen over again?

SONIA: *(Calling)* Hi Iris.

AMELIA: *(Hushed)* Why is she here?

SONIA: Open the door and ask her.

(Another knock)

IRIS: *(O S)* Just wanted to check in. I can come back another time.

SONIA: Open the door.

(AMELIA opens the door. IRIS steps inside.)

IRIS: I hope you don't mind that I stopped by. Some letters came to my agency for Sonia. From the ladies.

AMELIA: Ladies?

SONIA: I gave them Iris's address.

IRIS: It's better if they don't know where you live.

SONIA: We were just watching T V. There's been a plane crash on an island.

IRIS: *Lost!*

SONIA: Amy's a big fan.

AMELIA: Not that *big* of a fan.

IRIS: I was with them until the finale. They swore it wasn't purgatory and then low and behold...

AMELIA: It *wasn't*—you don't even— Okay, all of you who thought it was purgatory are basically idiots.

SONIA: Amy!

(AMELIA pauses Lost, *which goes against everything she stands for.)*

AMELIA: *(To IRIS)* I'm sorry, but look, they were alive. The season six, flash sideways, pushed the characters to answer unresolved questions in themselves. We were nearing the end of the series but the characters had not evolved to the point that the show could go off the air and leave the audience feeling settled. We would always worry about them. So they were never dead. They were never in purgatory! They were alive! And on that island trying to figure out their lives, their regrets, their futures! Shit. *(To* SONIA*)* I just ruined the whole thing for you!

IRIS: *(To* SONIA*)* You weren't kidding.

AMELIA: What?

SONIA: I told Iris, you know a lot about television.

AMELIA: It's what I'm into.

IRIS: It's good to have a passion. *(To* SONIA*)* I brought you a pie. Lemon meringue, your favorite.

SONIA: You're so thoughtful.

AMELIA: She won't be able to taste it.

IRIS: I thought the cold would at least feel good on your tongue.

SONIA: These meds are no joke. The inside of my mouth feels like a bomb went off.

AMELIA: I'll put it in the fridge.
(She goes to the kitchen.)

SONIA: Invite Ben over. We can have a dinner party.

(No response)

SONIA: Amy. Did you hear me? Call Ben.

AMELIA: *(O S)* Ben's…visiting his brother…in Connecticut.

IRIS: Oh yeah? I've got family there. What part?

*(*AMELIA *re-enters.)*

AMELIA: Um, Stars Hollow.

SONIA: What's he doing up there?

AMELIA: His brother Luke, um, owns a diner and needs an extra hand this week.

IRIS: Sounds like a good guy. Flying all the way across the country.

SONIA: You should have gone with him.

AMELIA: Who would take care of you?

SONIA: Don't worry about me. Live your life!

AMELIA: I'll get right on that.
(*She exits to the bedroom.*)

SONIA: I'm happy to see you. I've missed your face.

IRIS: I was here a week ago.

SONIA: It's been months.

IRIS: You're crazy.

SONIA: I'm drugged up. I haven't felt this psychedelic since the Seventies.

IRIS: Oh man, that was a good decade.

SONIA: I wish I would have known you then.

IRIS: I would have gotten you in a lot of trouble.

SONIA: Sounds all right to me. It would have been nice to have a friend back then.

IRIS: Do you want me to open some of the letters?

SONIA: Is there one from Varleen? She was having trouble with her new bunkmate.

IRIS: Which one is Varleen?

SONIA: The big lady. With good teeth.

IRIS: Right. She's a character.

SONIA: Isn't she? I was trying to get her to use better conflict resolution skills, but her first instinct is to fight. I'm afraid she'll end up in the hole.

IRIS: Those ladies really love you.

SONIA: Don't let me fool you. I had my share of enemies.

IRIS: Oh, hang on. Tamika had her baby! I'm a grandma!
(She pulls up a photo on her iPhone.)

SONIA: Oh, he's beautiful.

IRIS: Strong lungs too.

SONIA: You wouldn't know it now, but Amelia was a screamer. She could be fed, burped, changed—nothing wrong with that kid, and she would scream for hours.

IRIS: I remember those days with my two.

SONIA: Funny how she doesn't make much noise at all now. Comes home, makes dinner, and turns on the T V for the night.

IRIS: Give her a reason to turn off the T V.

SONIA: How can I? Look at me. *(Indicating the D V D cabinet)* Look in there.

(IRIS opens the D V D cabinet.)

IRIS: Oh wow! There are some good ones in here. *(Beat) Newhart! (Calling off excitedly.)* Amelia, you have *Newhart!*

(AMELIA runs from the bedroom.)

AMELIA: What happened?

IRIS: I didn't realize you could get this on D V D. / Boy this takes me back.

AMELIA: I thought she—

IRIS: What a great show. Maybe the *greatest.*

AMELIA: It ruined television finales for all time.
(She begins to head for her bedroom.)

IRIS: Why don't you stay out here with us?

AMELIA: That's okay. You guys can watch it though.

SONIA: I want to finish *Lost*—see if that pregnant girl is okay.

AMELIA: I already ruined the ending.

SONIA: I'm old. I'm high. I don't remember.

IRIS: I should be going anyway. *(Indicating the* Newhart *D V D)* May I?

AMELIA: Um. I don't really lend—

IRIS: I'm good for it.

SONIA: She can bring it back when she comes tomorrow.

AMELIA: Um…

IRIS: *(Overlapping)* I promise I'll return it.

AMELIA: Just don't like lose it—or damage it.

IRIS: You have my word. See you in a few days Sonia.

SONIA: See ya.

IRIS: Bye Amelia. Thanks.
(She exits.)

AMELIA: *(Calling off)* I'll know if you don't bring that back.
(Closing the door)
So like, are you a lesbian now?

SONIA: It's not like that. It's nice to have someone to talk to. I—I miss the ladies.

AMELIA: You can go back.

SONIA: I don't want to go back. But I still care about them.

AMELIA: How did she find you?

SONIA: When I found out I was sick, I wrote to her agency to see if they would help me get a letter to you.

AMELIA: To say what? "I'm dying. Thought you'd want to know."

SONIA: I figured you might have some questions about what happened. I wanted you to have the chance to ask whatever it is you need to ask.

AMELIA: And get you out.

SONIA: I didn't even know this was a possibility. I just wanted to start a dialogue.

AMELIA: A *dialogue*?

SONIA: It didn't come easily Amelia. I had to learn how to talk about what happened—and how to talk about him again.

AMELIA: You make it sound like what you did wasn't horrible. Like it's just something that you can talk out and it goes away.

SONIA: It's been a long time Amy.

AMELIA: Stop calling me that.

SONIA: I've been calling you Amy your whole life.

AMELIA: You haven't known me my whole life.

(Beat)

SONIA: Your dad wanted to name you Amy, but I told him that you needed a more mature name—for when you grew up.

AMELIA: And he named me Amelia.

SONIA: No. I chose it. He still insisted on calling you Amy.

AMELIA: No he didn't.

SONIA: It's been a long time. Memories get fuzzy.

AMELIA: I remember *everything* about dad. You're the one I'm trying to forget.

SONIA: Iris has offered to set us up with someone to talk to—

AMELIA: Like a therapist?

SONIA: Yes.

AMELIA: I don't need therapy.

(AMELIA *unpauses* Lost.)

SONIA: That's not what it looks like to me.

AMELIA: Let's get one thing straight. You can live here until you die, but you are no longer my mother. *(Re: Lost)* So this island, it's got like, mysterious healing powers.

(Transition)

Cupid

(The break room. AMELIA, BEN, and Plantasia are having lunch.)

BEN: If you won't go out to eat, let me at least *bring* you lunch.

AMELIA: I like what I make.

BEN: I can make that exact same thing for you.

AMELIA: Then what's the point?

BEN: Because it's not a date if I don't provide the lunch.

AMELIA: I never agreed to a date. I agreed to facilitate a lunch between you and Plantasia.

BEN: Okay…I'll just enjoy my chicken, fig and blue cheese wraps, pasta salad, and citrus spiced olives on my own.

AMELIA: You made all of that?

BEN: I'm a very good cook.

AMELIA: Why do you do that?

BEN: Do what?

AMELIA: You announce the things you're good at.

BEN: I do? (*Thinks*) I do! I suppose I believe it's okay to be aware of your strengths.

AMELIA: Aren't you afraid of sounding cocky?

BEN: Do I sound cocky?

AMELIA: No.

BEN: So then, no. (*Beat*) Try it.

AMELIA: No. I don't have anything to—no.

BEN: Come on. Name something you're really good at.

AMELIA: I really don't—

BEN: Okay, I'll be you. My name is Amelia and I am really good at…finding sponsor families for starving children in Burundi.

AMELIA: It's my job.

BEN: And you're really good at it.

AMELIA: They're starving children!

BEN: I should have invited them to lunch! Maybe they'd eat my food.

(*To shut* BEN *up,* AMELIA *takes a fig wrap and eats it.*)

AMELIA: (*Sincerely*) Oh wow. You *are* a really good cook.

BEN: See. I wasn't bragging, just stating a fact. Now it's your turn.

AMELIA: No…

BEN: You can do it. I believe in you. (*Beat*) My name is Amelia and I…

Kat Ramsburg   33

AMELIA: I—I'm really good at avoiding you all day.

BEN: Okay. Not exactly what I was going for, but since it's true I'll take it.

AMELIA: Sorry.

BEN: Sorry for avoiding me?

AMELIA: No. For—well, yeah, for that too.

BEN: Why do you avoid me?

AMELIA: I don't know. And I'm not saying that in the brush off way. I really *don't* know.

BEN: Some people take me the wrong way.

AMELIA: No. You're—

BEN: Because I'm just trying to be friendly. As far as friends go, I'm a catch.

(AMELIA *actually laughs at this.*)

BEN: I can't tell if you're laughing *at* me, or *with* me?

AMELIA: That's just a funny thing to say about yourself.

BEN: Well, it's true.

AMELIA: You remind me of someone on a sit-com. There's something not quite real about you.

BEN: *(Pinches himself)* Yup, still real. Who am I? Jim?

AMELIA: Jim?

BEN: Jim Halpert? *The Office.* Don't tell me you didn't watch *The Office.*

AMELIA: Of course I did. And rewatched it at least three times.

BEN: Me too.

AMELIA: But you're not Jim. He's too…mischievous.

BEN: But he got the girl.

(AMELIA *is embarrassed by this.*)

BEN: *(Covering)* Or maybe…Ross? Or Ted Mosby?

AMELIA: I loved *How I Met Your Mother*!

BEN: I'm more of a *Breaking Bad* kind of guy.

AMELIA: Oh yeah!! You're totally Walter Junior!

BEN: Flynn? I don't even get to be the lead of my own show?

AMELIA: But you get to live.

BEN: No, no, no, I'm Jesse Pinkman all the way. "Yeah bitch, magnets!"
(But he is too nice to be convincing.)

AMELIA: Hank. Final offer.

BEN: How about just Ben? Ben Sullivan.

AMELIA: Star of your own show. The guy people root for.

BEN: Sounds good to me.

AMELIA: Everything turns out alright for you.

BEN: I'm hoping so. *(Beat)* So…

AMELIA: So?

BEN: Why do you avoid me?

(Pause)

AMELIA: You…remind me that I'm not invisible.

BEN: That might be the nicest thing anyone has ever said to me.

(Beat)

AMELIA: Why did you talk to me? When did you—

BEN: Notice you? Let's see. I had been working here about…twelve minutes, when you walked by. I though you were absolutely… But I told myself, "Ben, you're new to Seattle, freshly divorced, and need to get your shit together before you think about talking to that woman." So that's what I did. I made myself better. Many of those lessons came from you, you know.

AMELIA: No…

BEN: Yes. Amelia, you're kind, and patient. Even when someone is chewing you out on the phone. The way you talk about the work we're doing here—like thirty-five dollars a month is actually providing these kids with a stable life. You know how to give everything of yourself while you're here, but I see the shift on the bus ride home. To a quieter place. It's peaceful there. And I like to imagine being there with you.

AMELIA: I'm sorry I didn't know you sooner.

BEN: I was invisible to you. But you're definitely not invisible to me.

AMELIA: It's not that I want to be. I just—I'm used to it. It's comfortable.

BEN: So be *un*comfortable for a couple minutes a day.

AMELIA: I'm uncomfortable right now.

BEN: Good! For thirty minutes today, you will be uncomfortable. When we have lunch tomorrow, it—

AMELIA: Tomorrow?

BEN: Did I forget to tell you? We're having lunch tomorrow. But only twenty-eight minutes will be uncomfortable. And then Thursday, only twenty-six minutes. By next month, you might even *enjoy* having lunch with me.

AMELIA: Now you're sounding cocky.

BEN: "I'm Amelia and I'm good at deflecting."

AMELIA: "I'm Ben and I'm good at…"

BEN: Yes?

(Beat)

AMELIA: I should get back to Burundi.

BEN: I really enjoyed our date.

AMELIA: It's not a—

BEN: It was a date.

(BEN *hugs* AMELIA. *She does not hug him back.*)

BEN: Ohhhh. I see we have something else to work on.

(AMELIA *pulls away.*)

AMELIA: Thanks for lunch.

BEN: See you tomorrow. *(The* How I Met Your Mother *joke:)* "It's going to be legen—wait for it—"

AMELIA: Okay. Tomorrow.
(She exits.)

BEN: *(Finishing the* How I Met Your Mother *joke.)* "—dary."

(Transition)

Prison Break

(AMELIA'*s apartment.* SONIA *is alone. She is watching* Orange is the New Black.)

SONIA: Tampon in a breakfast sandwich! We never had breakfast sandwiches.
(She continues to watch. Annoyed.)
We would have eaten you alive, Piper.
(She works to get out of bed. She begins to do very limited exercises; things she might have done in her cell.)
One. Two. Three. Four.
(She stops.)
No. That's it for today.
(She stands, doing nothing, in the way someone who is used to standing and doing nothing can.)

(Trying to remember.)
I pledge allegiance to the flag of the United Stages of American. And to the pre-public... The *R*epublic?
(Tries to remember)
Come on. You know this. The republican for which it stands. For liberty and for justice and for all. Okay. Okay. Not bad.
(She makes her way to the window and opens the curtain. The sun shines on her face and she smiles as though the world is perfect. She hums while trying to make her bed. She lines up her few belongings. She picks up the remote. Presses some buttons, but can't seem to get it to work.)
Damn D V R. I don't get you.
(She makes her way to the D V D cupboard.)
You want to talk about television, kid? You got it.
(Pulling down some D V Ds)
What's a "Buffy?" *Firefly?*
(Beat)
Only one season. Must not be too good.
(Beat)
Oh. *Friends.* That sounds nice.
(She selects Friends *and goes to the D V D player. She doesn't know how to make the machine work, gets frustrated, drops the D V D and bends down to pick it up. She falls.)*
Help! Amy? Amelia? Heeeeeelp! Hello? Someone! Help me!
(After a moment)
Guard!
(Transition)

Family Ties

*(*AMELIA*'s apartment. She has just returned from work.)*
SONIA: He just helped me back in to bed.

AMELIA: I don't want strangers in my home.

SONIA: You should know your neighbors, Am— Amelia. He works for a company called Amazon. Recently separated. Kind of handsome. His name is Raj. Not Roger, just Raj. He's Indian! Isn't that interesting?

AMELIA: No.

SONIA: He's been your neighbor for about six months and didn't know your name. So I told him all about you. You need more friends.

AMELIA: I have plenty of friends.

SONIA: You never talk about them. Who are they? They never come over. Or call.

AMELIA: Lorelai. She's an innkeeper. Mindy. She's a doctor. Philip and Elizabeth Jennings—I can't talk about what they do. Meredith. Liz. Leslie—

SONIA: And Raj, your handsome neighbor.

AMELIA: You should have called me.

SONIA: I couldn't get up. He heard me calling and climbed in through the window.

AMELIA: Convenient.

SONIA: If you didn't have Ben I'd set you two up.

AMELIA: Well, I do have Ben, so—

SONIA: I'd love to meet him.

AMELIA: You've made that very clear.

SONIA: I'd just like to know something about my daughter.

AMELIA: I live here. I go to work. I come home. I take care of you. Nothing else to know.

SONIA: Who took you to prom?

AMELIA: I didn't go to prom.

SONIA: Why not?

AMELIA: Prom's stupid.

SONIA: How old were you when you got your period?

AMELIA: Why would you want to know that?

SONIA: It seems like something a mother should know.

AMELIA: Twelve. I didn't know what it was, so I
thought I was dying for three months. *(Beat)* But then,
my foster mom—uh, she told me what was happening
and that I should be really proud. And that it was the
beginning of a lot of really wonderful things in my life.

SONIA: That was nice of her.

AMELIA: Yeah. She was the best. My *favorite* mom.

(Beat)

SONIA: Why didn't she try to adopt you?

AMELIA: It's none of your business.

SONIA: The state terminated my rights. You were free
for the taking.

AMELIA: They already had three kids. Money was tight.

SONIA: *(Very pointed)* And she only cared about you
because the state paid her to.

*(AMELIA picks up the remote and brings up the D V R.
She panics and eventually builds to a full teenage rage
meltdown.)*

AMELIA: What did you do?

SONIA: I don't know what you're—

AMELIA: Everything is gone!

SONIA: What's gone?

AMELIA: EVERYTHING. You erased my D V R!

SONIA: I don't know how to do that.

AMELIA: Well you did!

SONIA: I'll get them back for you.

AMELIA: You can't! They're gone!

SONIA: I just pushed some buttons.

AMELIA: Don't touch anything.

SONIA: I'm trying to learn all your T V shows!

AMELIA: Don't! They're *my* shows!

SONIA: Amy, I'm—

AMELIA: Stop calling me Amy! And stop trying to make me talk! And stop ruining every—. I should have never let you in here. I was fine without—
(She opens the D V D cupboard and pulls a couple out.)

SONIA: Then why did you?

AMELIA: Where else were you going to go?

SONIA: I never wanted to—

AMELIA: What? Have to deal with me again?

SONIA: Amelia, / no.

AMELIA: I'm sorry your plans didn't work out and only dad died.

SONIA: Don't say / that!

AMELIA: Trust me, I'm sorry you messed up too. Every. Single. Day.

(AMELIA puts a D V D in and presses play.)

SONIA: Don't say—Can you turn it off? For just a minute?

AMELIA: I want to watch T V!

(Beat)

SONIA: I wasn't a good mother to you. I know that.

AMELIA: Not exactly a news flash.

SONIA: But I got better, and there were women in there who never had a mother. I couldn't be a parent to you, so I tried to be one to them.

AMELIA: I'm glad they finally have a mother.

SONIA: You have one too, / Amelia.

AMELIA: No, I / don't. I don't need—

SONIA: Yes you do. Like it or not, I'm the one you got.

AMELIA: I don't remember you at all.

SONIA: Yes you do.

AMELIA: No, I—

SONIA: The good and the bad.

AMELIA: *(Finally taking her eyes off the T V)* What "good"? Most of the time you'd be staring at the wall like something was wrong with you.

SONIA: You don't know half of what was going on, kid. But if I could just tell you—

AMELIA: No! You don't get to change the story. Not when dad's not here to remind you how horrible of a mom and wife you were.

SONIA: You think you had it so bad, but you were damn lucky compared to the way I was raised.

AMELIA: Every time you try to defend yourself, it's like you're trying to erase my memories of him!

SONIA: I'll tell you anything you want to know.

AMELIA: I don't want *your* memories of him. I want my own.
(She goes back to the T V. After a beat.)

SONIA: He loved to listen to you sing.

AMELIA: You always said I was tone deaf.

SONIA: You were. Your dad didn't care. He would sit outside your room and listen to the concerts you would put on for your stuffed animals.

AMELIA: Because he was perfect.

SONIA: He wasn't perf—

AMELIA: Yes he was!

SONIA: He just figured out the parenting thing better than I did.

AMELIA: You could have just left.

SONIA: I should have. But now we have this second chance and—

AMELIA: No. No! That's not what this is. You're supposed to come here and die. You're supposed to be pathetic and sad and lonely. But you—you get letters! You say those people are your family! Why do *you* get a family!

SONIA: Because I learned to live again, Amy. And I want the same for you!

AMELIA: You don't deserve to be happy. You think that just because you were nice to some women that you get to go to The Good Place now? Well, *spoiler*: *It's NOT The Good Place!* And it's exactly where you belong!

SONIA: What are you talking about?

AMELIA: You deserve pain, and to be cut off from the world!

SONIA: I'm cut off from you—

AMELIA: You KILLED a person. You took away his life, but you get to keep yours. / That doesn't—

SONIA: Let's get one thing straight. I'm not here for your forgiveness. I just needed to see that I hadn't ruined *everything*. But baby, you are as good as dead. / Don't you see that? You are as good as dead.

AMELIA: Don't judge my life! You don't know what I've—

SONIA: Sometimes a mother has to make—

AMELIA: You are not my mother.

SONIA: Sometimes *a mother* has to make the hard decisions for her child / and that's what I'm going to do for you.

AMELIA: YOU ARE NOT MY MOTHER!

SONIA: I'm the only one you've got, kid. Now, you're going to go out there and make *real* friends.

AMELIA: I have *real*—

SONIA: You're going to find people to love and who love you back because that's what you deserve and that is what you are owed.

(AMELIA *turns up the volume on the T V as loud as she possibly can.*)

SONIA: I'm trying to talk to you!

SONIA:	AMELIA:
Please. Turn that off.	
	I'm watching this!
For one second!	
	No! It's my life.
I know! I know!	
	And I want to watch T V.
I'm just trying to—	
	I WANT TO
Just…	WATCH TV
Can we?	
I'm trying to talk to you!	
	NO! And I *have* real
	friends!
Amelia, I don't think—	Angela lives in
	Pittsburgh!

You need friends who—	Penny lives in Chicago!
I don't think they—	
	I don't care what you
	think!
Amelia, baby—	I *never* loved you.
	And you never loved me.
That's not	
True	It *is* true!
I'm learning how.	
	It's too late because
	I hate you! I hate you!
Shut up! I'm trying to love	I hate yooooooooooooou!
you.	
Shut up! Shut up!	I hate you!!!
You took me in!	
You wanted me here!	

AMELIA: I WANTED TO WATCH YOU DIE!

(Without missing a beat, SONIA *throws her bowl at the T V. The screen shatters. The T V is finally silenced.)*

(Transition)

Damages

*(*AMELIA *at work.)*

AMELIA: *(On the phone. Not on her game)* For thirty-five dollars a month, your child will receive nutritious food, a uniform for school, as well as community improvements that will help your child and her family, become self-sustaining. It's a really wonderful way to let a child know that someone out there knows she's alive, and wants the best for her. *(Listens)* I understand. If you'd prefer to sponsor an American child, I can transfer you to that depart— *(Listens)* But your tax dollars don't begin to— *(Listens)* I'm sure you do give

in other ways, but if you want to make a real impact
you have to say, *this* is the child I am supporting. *This*
child is the one I want to see thrive. Dropping off an
old coat at your dry cleaners each winter doesn't tell
a child that she deserves warm coat, shoes that fit,
food in her stomach, a roof over her head. Dropping
off your old coat means you have more room in your
closet for your Nordstrom addiction, something to
brag about to the moms at your play date, and worse,
it shows your own children that kids who don't have
families are not worthy of something new—something
that was chosen specifically for them, with love. They
are as disposable as your old winter coat. *(Listens)*
Hello?

*(*AMELIA *hangs up.* BEN *approaches.)*

BEN: Guess what?

AMELIA: Not now, Ben.

BEN: Okay, grumpy.

AMELIA: What do you want?

BEN: I would like for you to join me tomorrow night at
the Freemont Outdoor Movie. *Risky Business* is playing!
It's a real date. I will be purchasing the tickets, bringing
the picnic supplies, walking you home.

AMELIA: I can't. Netflix drops the new season of
Stranger Things tonight. And my T V is broken so I
have to go to the thrift store in the morning to—

BEN: Maybe you could watch it next weekend?

AMELIA: That's not—I have to binge it the first
weekend! I made a commitment to the show—to the
characters.

BEN: But wouldn't you rather hang out with a
handsome guy in real life than a bunch of pre-
pubescent tweens on T V?

AMELIA: If you begin something, you see it through. People who start a series and then give up on it because things get boring or the plot goes off the rails—they don't deserve to come back when times are good. Do you think I enjoyed Buffy's depression in season six?

BEN: You're upset about something.

AMELIA: Well done, Kojak.

BEN: Want to talk about it instead of insulting me in T V code?

AMELIA: No.

BEN: Do you want me to delete that last call from your records?

AMELIA: You heard?

BEN: (*Indicating a pod across the office*) I think they heard you all the way in Uzbekistan.

AMELIA: Shit.

BEN: We should really delete that call from your log.

(BEN *reaches over to* AMELIA *keyboard, enters a few things. He is very much in her personal space. She sort of doesn't mind.*)

AMELIA: Isn't that against the rules?

BEN: So is chewing out a donor. I figure manipulating the poorly designed program is far better than them being able to track the call back to you.

AMELIA: Thank you.

BEN: You're not going to tell me what's wrong?

AMELIA: It's…complicated.

BEN: I hope so. I just hacked the International Children's server. If all of that was for a banal grievance, I'm going to hesitate coming to your aid ever again.

AMELIA: It's not something I want to relive over and over.

BEN: Sounds like you need an escape. Like an outdoor movie. In Freemont. Tomorrow night.

AMELIA: You are persistent.

BEN: Yes I am.

(Beat)

AMELIA: Fine. Okay. Yes.

BEN: It's a date.

AMELIA: It's…a date.

(Transition)

Lie To Me

*(*AMELIA*'s apartment. The T V is gone.* SONIA *is asleep.* IRIS *is sitting on the couch reading.* AMELIA *comes out of the bedroom, dressed for her date.)*

AMELIA: Um…thanks for staying with her tonight.

IRIS: Happy to. It's much roomier in here without that T V. *(Beat)* It was an accident, sweetie.

AMELIA: No it— The movie is over around ten-thirty. I'll be home right after that.

IRIS: Sonia said you two had a good talk—before the T V.

AMELIA: Yeah, well, she's on a lot of drugs.

IRIS: She needs to know you're going to be okay.

AMELIA: I am going on a date tonight. I don't know if what I'm wearing is appropriate. I don't know how I'm supposed to behave, or when to laugh, and I have no idea how to flirt. I'm extremely nervous about what I'm going to talk about. I don't know if I'm supposed to let him pay, or if I should offer. If he tries to hold my hand, do I let him? When he walks me home... then what? I'm freaking out right now. I should have gone through this at sixteen, with my parents by my side. But instead I'm doing it in my thirties. Most likely I'll push Ben away. Or, like so many people in my life, he'll change his mind and get rid of me. So I don't know if I'm going to be okay.

IRIS: You told Sonia you've been dating Ben for a while. You met in a furniture store, right?

AMELIA: Yeah. Um. He's great.

IRIS: Have I ever told you about my kids?

AMELIA: The one in prison—

IRIS: And the doctor. They're about your age.

AMELIA: So?

IRIS: I wasn't the perfect mom, but there was one thing I was really good at—knowing when my kids weren't being honest with me. *(Beat)* Do you know what my daughter's favorite TV show is?

AMELIA: Empire?

IRIS: *Gilmore Girls*, which I didn't love. Would it have killed them to have a black family living in Stars Hollow? *(Beat) Stars Hollow*...the fictional town where the TV show takes place. And where a character named Luke, runs a diner. I don't recall him having a brother named Ben though. *(Beat)* I understand that your relationship with Sonia is complicated. But I also know that telling her stories about people on TV isn't helping her feel like she can move on.

AMELIA: I—I don't have any other stories.

(AMELIA and IRIS stare at each other at an impasse.)

AMELIA: You still gonna watch her or…

IRIS: I'll be here.

(AMELIA *begins to leave.*)

IRIS: *(Very gently)* Amelia? Let him pay. Laugh at his jokes, but only the ones you find funny. Make him feel like you are honored to be on a date with him, but always remember that he's the lucky one. Hold his hand, but nothing else on the first date. And you look lovely.

(Transition)

Perfect Strangers

(BEN *walks* AMELIA *home from a real date.*)

BEN: That wasn't so bad was it?

AMELIA: It was actually enjoyable.

BEN: Success!

AMELIA: I think I'm going to start going on lots of dates.

BEN: Wait a minute.

AMELIA: I wonder how many guys I can line up in a week.

BEN: None will really compare to me, so you might want to take it easy.

(AMELIA *and* BEN *reach her apartment.*)

AMELIA: Well, this is me. Um, thank you.

BEN: Thank *you.*

AMELIA: For being patient. For the date too—but mostly for being patient.

BEN: It was worth it.

(That awkward moment of not knowing how to end a first date.)

AMELIA: Okay. Well…

BEN: Yeah.

AMELIA: See you Monday.

(AMELIA turns to leave, but BEN grabs her and pulls her in to a hug. She doesn't hug back.)

BEN: This works better if you hug back.

(AMELIA half hugs BEN quickly and then stops.)

BEN: I don't mean to make you feel self-conscious but you have got to be the worst hugger on the planet.

AMELIA: I'm not used to—

BEN: I'm only pointing it out, because I'm a really great hugger and I'd be happy to teach you.

AMELIA: That's okay.

BEN: Oh, come on. Tonight was basically perfect. Let's go for a home run—and I mean that in the non-sexual way.

AMELIA: I'm not big on touching.

BEN: Oh, I am. I think hugs are just incredible. You can give them to family, or strangers. Children, or seniors. Seniors *LOVE* hugs. Homeless people—

AMELIA: You hug homeless people?

BEN: Sure! Not regularly, but yeah, if they look like they need one.

AMELIA: And they let you?

BEN: I've got a reputation. I'm a really good hugger. *(Pause)* Come here.

(AMELIA resists.)

BEN: Come here! Hugs don't hurt, Amelia.

(AMELIA *gives in.* AMELIA *and* BEN *stand facing each other, arms at their sides.*)

BEN: There's always confusion over the arms. Instinct is to alternate, one over, one under. That's a good hug for an acquaintance. Someone you wish to greet with a hug, but not linger in a hug. Make sense? *(Beat)* But the hugs I like best are the kind where two souls meet. And because our souls are buried deep inside of us, we have to squeeze together tight enough that they can find each other. Ready?

AMELIA: No.

BEN: Put your arms around me. *(Beat)* Come on. I smell really good.

(AMELIA *carefully wraps her arms around* BEN.)

BEN: You okay?

AMELIA: Yeah.

BEN: Now I put my arms around you.
(He slowly wraps his arms around her.)
Now we squeeze until we hear our souls say hello to each other.

(AMELIA *and* BEN *pull in to each other. They fit perfectly. She eventually relaxes in to it.*)

BEN: Hello.

AMELIA: Hello.

(After a moment)

BEN: Amelia, I want to date you. Officially. I don't want to pretend I'm stopping by to talk to Plantasia. I don't want to act like I'm not fighting for a seat next to you on the bus. I just want you. And me. I want us.

(Pause)

AMELIA: You don't want me, Ben. Believe me. You think you do, but my shelf life with people wanting me is not good. So let's not.

BEN: I say we do. I want to give it a shot. But I want something that is based on more than discussing the best television finale of all time.

AMELIA: *Six Feet Under.*

BEN: I want to date you.

AMELIA: You just like the idea of me. The enigma. But once you realize that there's not much more to me than this, you'll understand it was a mistake.

BEN: And what if the person I find is exactly who I've been looking for?

(Beat)

AMELIA: Most foster kids make up their life story. I don't think I ever met a kid who told the truth about how they got there. You never question anyone else's story. It's like, even if it's a lie, it belongs to that person, and that's probably the only thing they own, so you let them have it.

BEN: What's your story?

AMELIA: I'm disposable.

BEN: No offense, but I would've made up a happier story.

AMELIA: I'm not so good at making up happy stories on my own.

BEN: What if you let another character in?

AMELIA: Somehow you've made it through life with your heart still in tact. You're still hopeful that the world is a good place, full of optimistic people who fall in love and live happy lives. But I know how this ends. And the finale is never as satisfying as the series.

BEN: What if I promise you that if our series ends, I'll give you the best damn finale of your life? Flashbacks, flash forwards, reunions. People will be discussing us for years! Maybe we'll move on to other series, but people will always remember us from "Ben and Amelia." And I'll always say that was the best time of my life.

(Beat)

AMELIA: See you Monday.

BEN: Can I come in?

AMELIA: What? No! No. Did you think—?

BEN: No! We could watch some T V.

AMELIA: No, Ben. I'm really–

BEN: We'll be quiet.

(Beat)

AMELIA: Why would we need to be quiet?

BEN: Oh. Uh. Your neighbors. These apartments / have thin—

AMELIA: It's only eleven.

BEN: Yeah. No. I don't know why I said that.

AMELIA: I'm gonna go.

BEN: Okay. See I didn't—I don't want this to be weird. I know about your mom.

AMELIA: Excuse me?

BEN: It's not a big deal.

AMELIA: How do you—?

BEN: I Googled you.

AMELIA: Why would you do that?

BEN: It's what people do when they start dating. I assumed you Googled me too.

AMELIA: Why?

BEN: To learn more about you.

AMELIA: To see what you're getting in to?

BEN: Probably for some people. I was just looking for a way in.

AMELIA: Is that why you started talking to me? With that stupid plant.

BEN: No! I had been trying to build up the courage to talk to you for months!

AMELIA: You just wanted to meet the woman who killed her husband! Well go on up. She's in the living room.
(She starts to head the other direction.)

BEN: Come back. Amelia!

AMELIA: No!

BEN: Just listen for a second.

AMELIA: Did you ever think that there might be a reason I don't talk about it? Did you—shit—did you tell everyone at work?

BEN: No! I promise!

AMELIA: Did everything make sense once you learned what I came from?

BEN: Sort of. No. I guess.

AMELIA: What does that mean?

BEN: I stopped reading. It wasn't my business.

AMELIA: You're right. It's not.

BEN: And I thought, one day, you would tell me what you wanted me to know.

AMELIA: You don't need to know anything. Go home Ben.

BEN: Don't do this!

AMELIA: Just go!
(She runs in the direction of her apartment.)
(Transition)

The Facts Of Life

(As much as possible, this scene should toggle effortlessly between the two locations as it would if we were watching it on television.)

(IRIS stands near the door. AMELIA hangs her coat.)

AMELIA: Thanks again.

IRIS: How did it go?

AMELIA: Exactly how I thought it would.

IRIS: First dates are always awkward. Think about giving it another chance.

(AMELIA is not in the mood to be mothered.)

IRIS: See you in the morning.

AMELIA: Sure.

(IRIS exits. AMELIA puts a blanket over SONIA. She tucks the blanket all around her, like a burrito, or a mummy. SONIA stirs.)

SONIA: Your dad used to tuck you in like that.

AMELIA: I remember.

SONIA: He was a good father.

AMELIA: Yeah, he was.

SONIA: We didn't want kids, but you showed up, and something just took over with your dad. He knew what to do. People say you just instinctively know. I never did.

(Outside AMELIA*'s apartment.* BEN *sits on the curb, not having left from the date. Iris approaches.)*

IRIS: Sir, are you okay?

BEN: Bad ending to a great date.

IRIS: Ah. You must be Ben.

BEN: They guy who never gets the girl.

IRIS: Iris. Amelia and Sonia's—friend. It's nice to finally meet you.

BEN: You've heard about me?

IRIS: We've heard a few stories. You name your plants, right?

BEN: I do! Amelia told you that?

IRIS: Oh, yes. She's told Sonia all about you.

(Back in AMELIA*'s apartment. She brings* SONIA *her meds.)*

SONIA: When I found out you were a girl, I thought it might be nice—a built in best friend. But you came and all you wanted was to be outside in the mud with your dad.

AMELIA: You could have come.

SONIA: It felt better to feel sorry for myself—watching this perfect little family that didn't want anything to do with me.

AMELIA: You didn't want anything to do with us.

SONIA: I felt used. Like you had hid in my womb, stolen my body for a time, then ran off with your father. He had been mine before you came.

AMELIA: *(She finally decides to ask.)* Is that why you did it? You resented him?

SONIA: It's not that simple.

AMELIA: The psychiatrists reports said you were depressed. But there are lots of depressed people / who don't—

SONIA: You read the reports?

AMELIA: When I turned eighteen. They didn't give me a lot of details before then. I remembered us driving to the game, then waking up in a hospital. I overheard the social worker talking to a nurse. That's when I figured out you were in jail and that dad was dead.

SONIA: I wish they would've let me talk to you after— when I started getting better. At least I could have tried to be a parent to you.

AMELIA: The whole point is that you didn't want to be one.

(On the stoop.)

BEN: I think she's worth it. But I—I just don't know if *she* sees that. And I don't know if I'm enough of a person to show her.

IRIS: You're the first person willing to give it a shot. That says a great deal about you.

(AMELIA's apartment.)

SONIA: No one teaches you how to be in a family. We're all just thrown into one and expected to survive it. *(Beat)* It was Varleen who—

AMELIA: I don't want to hear about your prison friends.

SONIA: She was up for parole, but her anger—whew! Rages like you've never seen. All the other ladies— they walked around her like she was a bomb about to go off. But I sought her out. I asked why she was so angry. I don't know what made me do it. And I don't know why she opened up to me.

AMELIA: And that makes you a mother?

SONIA: It was a start. *(Beat)* It was that moment that I felt the instincts kick in.

AMELIA: It's not *instinct*. It's called *unconditional* love.

(On the stoop)

IRIS: Bringing them back together felt like a good plan. I convinced myself, here are two people who desperately want to be loved by the other person. This seems obvious. But these last couple of months have been…I'm not sure it was the right decision for either one of them.

(AMELIA's apartment.)

SONIA: We were heading down the freeway. You were mad we would be late to your soccer game. Your dad was trying to calm you down. It was loud and—I don't know—I just needed it to stop.

AMELIA: You left a suicide note. You *knew* you were going to do it.

SONIA: But I changed my mind. I was driving towards the underpass. My foot was on the accelerator. And something inside me kept screaming "Stop! Stop it Sonia!"

AMELIA: It was dad!

SONIA: No. It was inside of me. All of a sudden I realized what I had was good. I wasn't perfect, but I could be better.

(The stoop)

IRIS: Maybe it's a flaw in our design—needing to be part of a family. A useless remnant from the prehistoric age when we had to form tribes to survive.

BEN: It's not useless. It's the only thing holding us together.

(AMELIA's apartment)

SONIA: I slammed on the breaks.

AMELIA: But it was too late.

SONIA: It kept you alive.

AMELIA: And you.

SONIA: I turned the wheel to try to avoid the underpass—

AMELIA: I read the police report—

SONIA: But we were too close and the passenger side hit—

AMELIA: I said, I read the report!

SONIA: I just want you to know that I tried to stop.

AMELIA: You could have turned the wheel the other way. Saved dad.

SONIA: I didn't think—

AMELIA: A *real* mother would have sacrificed herself!

SONIA: I know that now.

(Transition)

Arrested Development

(AMELIA's apartment. Later)

(She takes a long look at a sleeping SONIA. SONIA is clearly having trouble breathing. AMELIA turns up the oxygen. SONIA stirs.)

SONIA: *(Somewhat incoherently)* It's a girl?
Amelia.
We'll call her Amelia.

(Transition)

Twilight Zone

(The next morning. AMELIA *is asleep on the couch.* SONIA *is in bed but rather alert. She and* IRIS *are looking at Iris's phone.)*

AMELIA: *(Groggy)* What time is it?

IRIS: Nine-thirty.

AMELIA: Crap.

SONIA: Morning, Amelia.

IRIS: Long night?

AMELIA: Yeah. She had hallucinations. Erratic breathing. When did you get here?

IRIS: About an hour ago.

SONIA: We're looking at pictures of celebrities with no eyebrows.

AMELIA: You're sitting up.

SONIA: I feel great.

AMELIA: *(To* IRIS*)* Did she take her meds?

SONIA: I'm right here.

AMELIA: Did you take your / meds?

SONIA: No I did not. They make me feel fuzzy. I'd like to go for a walk.

IRIS: Oh…I don't know / about that.

SONIA: You've been bugging me to go outside. So let's go outside.

IRIS: How about I open the curtains? Let the sun–

SONIA: When is Ben coming?

AMELIA: Not today.

SONIA: I feel well enough to meet him. Let's have him over.

IRIS: Sonia…

SONIA: Call him Amelia! We can order a pizza if no one feels like cooking.
(She tries to get up.)

IRIS: Whoa. Where're you going?

SONIA: *(She's a different, harder woman)* For my afternoon walk. We go outside from two to three p.m. Rain or shine. Did the rules change? You guys have to tell us these things. You know Varleen gets pissed when you change the rules and don't tell us. I know you don't like it when Varleen goes on one of her rampages.

IRIS: We're going to stay inside today.

AMELIA: *(To IRIS)* It's not usually this bad.

SONIA: I've got rights! Twenty-three hours in, one out!

AMELIA: *(To IRIS)* Usually it's just a lot of mumbling.

IRIS: It's not two P M yet Sonia.

SONIA: "Sonia?" When did you start talking to me like I was a human being?

IRIS: Come and lay back down.

SONIA: VARLEEN! They're taking away rec time! Stay calm Varleen! We've got rights! We'll get to the bottom of this! Varleen? Varleen? JUST. STAY. CALM!
(She tries her best to bang on the bars of the bed.)
Gimme my rec time! I GOT RIGHTS.

(IRIS does her best to calm SONIA while AMELIA slips morphine under her tongue.)

SONIA: Don't put that shit in my mouth you mother fucker!

(IRIS scoops it up and puts it back in SONIA's mouth trying to let it dissolve.)

IRIS: Sonia. Shhhhh. It's Iris and Amelia here. You're home. You're here with me and your daughter, remember. Shhhhh.

(*Eventually* SONIA *calms down and falls asleep.*)

AMELIA: Her hallucinations are never that vivid.

IRIS: Sometimes, close to the end, they experience one last burst of energy.

AMELIA: Like with McSteamy.

IRIS: It's going to be soon Amelia.

(*Pause*)

AMELIA: What do we do?

IRIS: You say what you need to say. (*Beat*) Do you want me to stay?

AMELIA: No.

IRIS: Call me if you need *anything.* You have the hospice number?

AMELIA: Yeah.

IRIS: I'll check in in a few hours.
(*She exits.*)

SONIA: (*She's another woman.*) Damn it Steve! Don't slam the door!

AMELIA: Iris had to go home for a little bit.

SONIA: Hurry up and get dressed, Amy. We're gonna be late for your soccer game.

(*Transition*)

The Series Finale

(AMELIA's *apartment.* SONIA *is in bed. Her breathing is erratic and labored. She is in and out of consciousness.*)

AMELIA: So, um…that makes nine foster homes. Then I was in a couple of group homes. Some good. Some bad. There's this weird hierarchy with foster kids. The ones whose parents are dead, from drugs or being murdered or something, they get sympathy. But those of us who are in the system because our parents are in prison, we're garbage. So I just kind of did my own thing. Nobody cared where I was, or who I was with…I just walked around Seattle until I turned eighteen.

(AMELIA *sits up to check on* SONIA. *Still sleeping*)

AMELIA: What else?

(*Pause*)

I thought I was gay for a while. I was obsessed with girls—women actually. I found myself staring at them and so I thought, "I guess I'm gay." I tried being with this one girl who I met at a shelter. But she just needed someone to make sure she ate every few days, and I needed someone to care if I came home at night. Then I realized I wasn't looking at the women sexually, you know? I was studying them. Trying to learn how to be a woman. What was I supposed to look like? How was I supposed to talk? Someone is supposed to teach you that stuff. Like how to shave your legs. What color lipstick looks good. That kind of thing.

(*Beat*)

I didn't have that…influence, growing up so…

(*Long pause*)

I don't know what you want to know.

(*Long pause*)

I don't know what you need to hear.

(Long pause)

SONIA: Ben.

AMELIA: You're awake?

SONIA: More Ben. I want to meet him.

AMELIA: Oh. Well…

SONIA: Aiden makes furniture.
Sex and the City.

Roseanne taught you
about your
period.

I've watched
a lot
of T V
lately.

(SONIA takes AMELIA's hand. AMELIA lets her.)

SONIA: Iris
said
Ben is nice.

AMELIA: Yeah. He is.

SONIA: Tell me
about *him.*
The one Iris met.

AMELIA: Um. I… I don't really know him very well.

SONIA: He likes you?

AMELIA: Yes.

SONIA: You like him?

AMELIA: I want to.

SONIA: Then do.

AMELIA: It's not that simple. He…

SONIA: Likes you.
Start there.

(AMELIA *considers this.*)

SONIA: Turn up
oxygen

I can't

breathe.

AMELIA: Are you okay? What do you want me to—?

SONIA: Sometimes
people
see past what
we see in
ourselves.

I really

I can't

breathe.

AMELIA: The oxygen is as high as it will go.

(SONIA *is taking her final breaths. They get further and further apart, until they finally stop.* AMELIA *holds her hand through all of it.*)

AMELIA: Mom? Mom?

(For a while AMELIA watches SONIA's body.

(*After a moment, there is a quiet knock at the door.* AMELIA *pulls herself together, and goes to open the door.*)

(*It's* BEN. *She rushes into his arms. He hugs her back.*)

(Blackout)

END OF PLAY

APPENDIX

A Key to the Unexplained Television References

"My friends, Lily and Marshall, used to live here."
— *How I Met Your Mother*

"Like I'm Izzie Stevens, or something!"
—The gullible doctor on *Grey's Anatomy.*

"I, um, lived with this family once. The Banks's. They were super rich. And their nephew, Will, lived there too. He was from West Philadelphia. Born and raised."
—*The Fresh Prince of Bel-Air*

"I walked in to his store and I saw him. He was wearing a blue denim shirt. And his dog ran up to me and started, uh, humping my leg."
—Carrie and Aidan's meet-cute, *Sex and the City*

"Stars Hollow"
— *Gilmore Girls*

"His brother Luke, um, owns a diner…"
— *Gilmore Girls*

"Or maybe…Ross?"
— *Friends*

"Lorelai. She owns an inn. Mindy. She's an OBGYN. Philip and Elizabeth Jennings, but I can't talk about what they do. Meredith. Liz. Leslie."
— *Gilmore Girls (Lorelai), The Mindy Project (Mindy), The Americans (Philip and Elizabeth), Grey's Anatomy (Meredith), 30 Rock (Liz), Parks & Rec (Leslie)*

"…she told me what was happening and that I should be really proud. And that it was the beginning of a lot of really wonderful things in my life."
—Rosanne telling Darlene about her period on *Roseanne*

"You think that just because you were nice to some women that you get to go to the Good Place now? Well, SPOILER: IT'S NOT THE GOOD PLACE."
—Sorry if I just spoiled the first season of *The Good Place* for you…

"Angela lives in Pittsburgh! Penny lives in Chicago!"
—*My So Called Life (Angela), Happy Endings (Penny)*

"Like with McSteamy."
— *Grey's Anatomy*

www.ingramcontent.com/pod-product-compliance
Lightning Source LLC
Chambersburg PA
CBHW052214090426
42741CB00010B/2542